The ABCs of Home Buying:
15th Anniversary Edition

by
Marc Zirogiannis

Zirogiannis, Marc
The ABCs of Home Buying: 15th Anniversary Edition
112 pages

ISBN: 978-1-329-40347-5

Red Flag Advisors, Inc.
338 Jericho Tpke-Ste 114
Syosset, NY 11791

Inquiries or additional information contact
redflagadvisors@gmail.com or visit our website:
www.marczirogiannis.com

Printed in the United States of America

THIS BOOK IS DEDICATED TO MY BOYS

About The Author

Marc Zirogiannis holds a B.A. from Long Island University and a *Juris Doctor* from Hofstra University's School of Law. Mr. Zirogiannis is a world renowned Business Development Consultant and Author. Mr. Zirogiannis has practiced the martial arts for over 25 years and earned a 2nd Dan under the supervision of Grandmaster Y.H. Park in Levittown, New York. He has been active in practicing and teaching meditation for 10 years. He has published numerous books, eBooks, and Audio Books an on a variety of subjects, and, is currently the lead correspondent for *Tae Kwon Do Times*, an international print publication. He lectures on a variety of topics, including business development, personal development, and matters of the martial arts.

His novella, **Hitler's Orphan: Demetri of Kalavryta,** has won critical acclaim and been the subject of a radio program. It is currently in negotiations to become the basis of a more extensive work.

His latest work **The Suffering of Innocents** (2015) was released by *Revival Waves of Glory Books & Publishing* and has been a critical success.

Acknowledgements

Thanks to 15 years of book readers and home-buyers for encouraging and supporting the prior versions of this publication. I am truly humbled by the support. After years of publishing numerous, varied works it is amazing that the original version of this work is still the best seller.

Thanks to my dear friend and fellow author, John Gallagher, for his encouragement and integrity. He has always remained painfully honest in the review of my work.

Finally, thanks to Ms. Tiffany Sabal in formatting, typing and assisting in the painstaking job of recreating this text.

Marc A. Zirogiannis

THE ABCs OF HOME BUYING:
15th Anniversary Edition

2015 Introduction

In 2000 I released the original version of **The ABCs of Home Buying: A Practical Guide.** The original release was a labor of love for me and was designed to guide my, then client base, through the rigors of the home buying process. It was designed to demystify the process.

The success of the book was a pleasant surprise. It quickly became the #1 Real Estate book on **Amazon** and stayed on the top for some time. The book was also a critical success. The book was favorably reviewed by Joe Catalano, the famous Real Estate reporter, as well as others in the field, for its sensible and practical advice for lay people engaged in the home buying process. It led, for me, to an adjunct faculty position at Hofstra University, a series of other books, including a **Second Edition**, and numerous lectures. It was a success by all accounts.

Fast forward to 2015. I am no longer engaged in the practice of law yet the demand for the book has not waned. People still write me to tell me how much they valued this companion to their important purchase. One reader even wrote me that despite the age of the work it "still offered me everything I needed about understanding the process and the questions I needed to ask."

It was because of this demand that I decided it was the right time to release an Anniversary edition of the book to make it easier to obtain than the "out of print" editions published years ago.

So, essentially, unaltered but for some date modifications and slight revisions I hope you find this work as valuable as readers have for the past 15 years.

2000 Edition Introduction

The late 1990s marked the most resurgent Real Estate Sales Market in modern history. Fueled mostly by a thriving economy the demand for houses exceeded the supply. Sellers were actually able to set sales prices for their homes with the expectation that their asking price would be the opening bid for their sale, rather than the ceiling. Fair market values for houses increased by 20 to 30 percent in only several years. The Internet has been an important tool, not only for the buying and selling of houses, but for the providing of all services associated with the process. All of these factors served, and still serve, to make the process of shopping for, and buying a house, more confusing and laden with pitfalls than ever before.

The purchase of a house is the single most important financial undertaking of an individual's existence. In New York the average house costs more than four times the average salary earned by individuals in the state. An individual may spend upwards of 30 percent of his or her income on monthly housing expenses.

This sum factors in only the direct cost associated with the acquisition of the house; there are untold financial commitments associated with maintenance of a house, both after the acquisition and over the life of your stay there.

It is for all these reasons that I felt compelled to write a straightforward guidebook to the home buying experience. I strove to prepare a practical handbook that would simplify this complex process utilizing the knowledge and experience I have gained in working in a field that I truly love: Real Estate. This book is designed to be used both as an overview to the entire home buying process, and as a specific guide to the individual topics highlighted within.

You may find yourself reading this book once in its entirety before fully engaging in your home buying venture, and then, referring to it at various times throughout your journey as specific topical questions come to mind. It is my greatest hope that in reflecting on the entire process long after you have settled into your lovely new home, you will feel that the process was made easier knowing you had the comfort of this book to guide you. Until that time, happy house hunting.

Chapter 1:   To Buy or To Rent?

Several years ago I sat in my beautiful garden apartment contemplating whether or not to renew my lease for another year. I took into account several factors: the increase in rent, the need for maintenance on my apartment, and the prospect of expanding my family. I ended up asking myself the same question so many other people ask themselves everyday: "should I think about buying a house of my very own?"

Although home ownership is part and parcel of the American Dream, it is not, of course, an inalienable right. It is not attainable by every individual, nor is it desirable to everyone. In determining whether or not home ownership is right for you, and more significantly, if it is right for you right now, you must ask yourself a number of questions. These are questions in which there are no right or wrong answers. These are questions that are so fact sensitive that although two very similar individuals with similar lifestyles, from similar walks of life, of similar age and sensibility may arrive at the same ultimate conclusion for very different, and very personal reasons.

For some, the decision to buy a house is based upon some of the practical advantages that home ownership affords you. It affords you the opportunity, for little more than the price of your average apartment rental, to own a full-fledged home. Unlike your monthly rental payment which offers has no long-term value; every month when you mail your mortgage payment, you are building equity that you will retain later on when you decide to "buy up" to a bigger house, or to liquidate when you retire. Additionally, every dollar you spend on repairs and renovations benefits you directly, rather than your landlord. This is one of the most practical and most cited reasons for people buying their own house rather than renting.

Buying a house also affords the homeowner certain tax advantages that the rental option does not have. Your mortgage interest, in the event of mortgage financing, has tax deductibility advantages, which helps offset your income and lower your tax burden. The same is true of the Real Estate taxes associated with living in your home. Major repairs also play a part in tax savings, depending on the circumstances, in the current tax year, or upon the sale of your home in offsetting your taxable gain.

While some appreciate and benefit from the practical advantages of home ownership, most homebuyers agree that home ownership is fulfillment of their pursuit of the American Dream. It is a tangible expression of the fruits of their labor for many years to provide for their family. It is their opportunity to live in an idyllic community with a white picket fence and a yard to let their children run freely. It is something they can proudly call their own.

However, there are some people who will choose the rental option over buying, hands-down. For the majority of those individuals it is a matter of simple economics. They have been unable or unwilling to accumulate the capital necessary to serve as a down payment plus the closing costs. For others it is a deliberate decision to keep their lives as unencumbered as possible.

There are advantages to the rental option: you are often not responsible for the significant maintenance associated with home ownership. The responsibility for major repairs and upkeep falls with the Landlord, affording the tenant the luxury of utilizing their free time and discretionary income for pursuits other than changing the pipe under the sink when it leaks.

Others choose the rental option because it offers them flexibility, within the confines of their lease agreement, to relocate at any time, to any place they choose, without the major consequences associated with the sale of a home.

When I evaluated my personal circumstances at the time I considered renewing my lease I knew that the right decision for me was to commence looking for a house to purchase. Although I loved my apartment and have very fond memories of my times there, it was time for me to afford myself the benefits of home ownership. I was looking to expand my family and needed more room than my apartment afforded. The monthly carrying costs associated with moving into a bigger apartment would probably have exceeded my monthly mortgage payments with no long-term benefits. Finally, the tax advantages of home ownership would help offset any increase in income due to the expansion of my Real Estate practice.

There is no right or wrong answer to the question of whether home ownership is for you. However, there is fault in not carefully considering the questions associated with making the decision to buy or continue to rent. It is important to not let the desire to fulfill the dream obstruct you from honestly assessing your personal and financial circumstances before making one of the most important decisions of your life.

Advantages and Disadvantages of Buying and Renting

BUYING

Advantages
Tax Benefits
Build Equity

Disadvantages
Taxes Can Go Up

RENTING

Advantages
No Upkeep
No repairs
Flexibility

Disadvantages
No Tax Benefit
No Equity
Restrictions (i.e. No Pets)

Chapter Notes

Chapter 2:   What Can I Afford?

So, you've decided to go forward and buy a home of your very own. You spend time looking in the Real Estate section of the local newspaper, searching the Internet, and looking at houses with Real Estate Agents. After seeing more houses than you can count you stumble upon just the house you were looking for: four bedrooms, three-and-a-half baths, eat-in kitchen with full dining room, central air conditioning, cathedral ceilings, built-in Olympic-size swimming pool, and two acres of land in one of the best school districts on the North Shore of Long Island. The Real Estate Agent compliments you on your taste, and tells you what a steal this house is. "And," she adds, "I think I can get the owner to practically give it away for $1.2 million, since you're such a lovely couple."

After regaining consciousness, it is at this point that you must decide whether to head for the door, negotiate the price further, or to look no further and make an offer.

The question before you is, simply put, "Can I afford this house?" For someone who has never purchased a home the question of knowing what you can afford is not an easy one. In the above example, if you and your spouse make a combined, respectable, income of $60,000, the chances are that the house in question is out of range of your financial wherewithal. The problem is, in reality, that most choices will not be as obvious as the one presented here. You must determine what you can afford before you commence the search for a house to buy. This will save you from wasting your own time, the time of the Real Estate professionals, and the time of the homeowner. More importantly, it will save you from the disappointment of finding your "dream house" and being unable to consummate the transaction. It is extremely unpleasant, and sometimes costly, to discover weeks or months into the process that the house you are in contract to purchase is not the one you can afford.

For the sake of clarity, you should understand the question, "What can I afford?" is not the one that has a concrete answer. You will not come to the conclusion that you can afford a house for $351,323.72 and not a penny more. What will happen, however, after considering certain factors, is that you will determine a price range of homes you can afford. Then you can begin sensibly and efficiently looking for a house that you will, clearly, be able to purchase, if you so desire.

In my parents' generation people often determined what they could afford utilizing a common sense approach. They looked at their financial situation at the time they were looking to buy, including such factors as: how much money they saved for a down payment and how much they were making over the next several years following the purchase. They then looked at coworkers, family, and people similarly situated financially to evaluate the neighborhoods where they resided. This method gave them a rough idea of what they believed they could afford, and they started searching in that price range.

The rule of thumb at one time was: **one week's salary to pay the mortgage**. This approach still has tremendous merit. It is the fundamental starting place for determining what you can afford, because no one can know your financial situation, and your earning potential, better than you. The problem with this approach is that, because it leaves a large margin for error or miscalculation, there is still the likelihood that you cannot afford the property you are seeking to buy and the deal may fall through. Still, it is important to start with this technique.

While no approach is foolproof, you want to reduce to the smallest possibility the chances that your deal will fall apart midstream. In my opinion, the best way to determine what you can afford is to begin with the method our parents used and to augment it with the expertise and experience of a mortgage professional.

In the next chapter I will discuss the differences between the various types of mortgage professionals; however, for the purposes of this discussion any competent mortgage professional will suffice. The use of a mortgage professional can help you realistically determine the price range of homes you should be shopping for. This mortgage professional will use your personal data with the potential data associated with a prospective property and the current market temperament (i.e. interest rates). They will analyze your income, your credit, your savings, and whatever factors are associated with the generally accepted mortgage underwriting guidelines to help you determine what you can reasonably afford in the way of a house. This professional will help you factor in the cost of Real Estate Taxes, Homeowners Insurance, Loan Principal, and Interest, to help you determine which monthly housing payment you can afford.

The benefits of this approach are twofold: it will keep you from being disappointed as you shop for a house and it will keep you from undertaking a financial commitment that will ultimately encumber you so much financially that even though you might be able to buy the house you select, you couldn't possibly maintain the house for any period of time.

I would advise all first-time homebuyers to utilize a mortgage professional to help determine what they can afford. This is true even of buyers who are fortunate enough to be able to purchase a property with substantial cash down payment, or even those who intend to buy "all cash". The information past buyers have gathered from these professionals is invaluable.

You should understand that just because you consult a mortgage professional to assist you in determining what you can afford, you are not obligated to utilize that professional in obtaining the actual financing. You are free to shop around at any time. A competent mortgage professional will be glad to consult with you, initially at low or no cost, in the hopes of building a relationship with you that might last many years.

There is an additional advantage to seeing a mortgage professional to determine what you can afford before you get started shopping for a house. Today's seller, like today's buyer, is very sophisticated. They do not want to take their property off the market for a time to discover weeks later that the buyer cannot afford to consummate the deal and that they have lost potential opportunities to sell. Therefore, it is standard to request a pre-qualification or pre-approval letter for the buyer before the seller will go to contract. In fact, some Real Estate Agents will not even allow a binder to be signed unless the buyer has seen a mortgage professional and had their individual circumstances reviewed and qualified. You can save yourself the possibility of losing a bid on the "house of your dreams" because another potential buyer showed up at the open house with a pre-qualified letter and you have yet to see a mortgage professional.

Let's take a quick moment to review what the first two steps in the home buying process are: the decision to buy, and the exploration of how much you can afford. These factors both lend themselves to deliberate contemplation on the part of the buyer. Once you have found a house that you love and that you can afford, the process shifts into high gear.

Before you visit a mortgage professional, you might want to gather the following documents:

-Prior Two (2) Years Tax Return   (State   and Federal)
-Prior Year's W-2 Form or 1099
-Prior Two (2) Weeks Pay Stubs
-Prior Twelve (12) Months Bank Statements
-Recent Credit Report If You Have One
-Any Explanation or Proof For Credit Blemishes

These documents will help your mortgage professional determine your eligibility for a variety of mortgage programs.

How Much Home Can You Afford?

Annual Gross Income: **[$50,000]**
Mortgage Amount You Can Support: **[$152,698]**
Mortgage Interest Rate: **[7.25]**
Down Payment Percentage: **[10.30%]**
Length of Mortgage (In Years): **[30]**
Price of Home You Can Afford: **[$170,198]**
Down Payment Amount: **[$17, 500]**
Monthly Mortgage Amount: **[$1,041.67]**
% Of Income to Dedicate: **[25%]**

There are many computer programs that will help you figure out how much you can afford to spend on a house before you go shopping. In this scenario, the buyer has plugged in their current income, the current interest rate, the amount they have saved for a down payment, and the amount of their income they feel they can dedicate to their housing costs. The program responds by providing them with a proposed house that is affordable with the correlating mortgage amount necessary to complete the transaction.

Chapter Notes

Chapter 3:   The Players

One of the things that makes the home buying experience so interesting, yet simultaneously so complicated, is that in a relatively short period of time (two to four months) your circle of friends and acquaintances will grow by almost two dozen. There are so many people involved in your deal that you need a veritable playbill to keep track of who all the players are, how much they will cost, and what purpose they serve.

The following is a list of many players who will be involved in your purchase. Some you may never even meet, even though you may pay for their services. Others listed may not apply to your particular transaction, depending on what role they play.

THE REAL ESTATE AGENT—While many buyers look for homes that are being sold directly by homeowners, most still utilize the services of a Real Estate Agent to help them find a prospective residence. A qualified Real Estate Agent is in the best position to help meet the need and abilities of a buyer. The Real Estate Agent of the buyer can utilize their experience and extensive database to help locate a house that meets the specified requirements of the buyer. The Real Estate Agent will make appointments to see the prospective homes and help initiate the negotiations on the terms and conditions of the eventual contract. The Real Estate Agent should be a buffer between you and direct contact with the seller, which will make the awkwardness of expressing some of your concerns about the house much less difficult.

The Real Estate Agent will also serve the function of being available to meet many of the various professionals and inspectors at the house after you decide to go forward with the purchase. By having the Real Estate Agent meet the termite inspector or appraiser at the house you will save time at a point in your life when you need to maximize your income.

Many people have the misconception that all Real Estate Agents are high-pressure salespeople who are only interested in locking in a commission. My experience is that most Real Estate Agents are hard working professionals who genuinely like people and like the business they are in. Of course, they are salespeople, but they only have as much power as you allow them to exert. If a Real Estate Agent is not showing you houses that meet your requirements, such as your price range, or if your Real Estate Agent is exerting uncomfortable pressure that makes you feel awkward about proceeding with the transaction, you should consider finding one that makes you feel more comfortable. *In New York the buyer does not have to pay any fee to the Real Estate Agent; all fees are borne by the seller.*

THE MORTGAGE PROFESSIONAL—As was discussed earlier in this book, the mortgage process will be paramount to the entire real estate transaction. There are two (2) basic types of mortgage professionals that exist; they are the Mortgage Banker and the Mortgage Broker. There is tremendous misunderstanding among the general public about the role served by each and the advantages to utilizing the services of one as opposed to the other. **Let's start by defining each:**

A.   THE MORTGAGE BANK—The Mortgage Bank is a direct lender. When you apply for a loan through a Mortgage Bank you are applying with the institution that will be advancing the money for the purchase of your home. This Bank might be a conglomerate, multi-million dollar entity like Citibank or Chase that provides a variety of services ranging from the provision of savings and checking accounts to mortgage originations; or the bank could be a smaller, independent, licensed Mortgage Bank that provides only the services or originating mortgage loans.

B.   THE   MORTGAGE   BROKER—The Mortgage Broker is an entity that arranges loans through third party lenders. In other words, when you apply for a loan with the Mortgage Broker he does not advance the money himself, he shops it around to various lenders, some of whom you could also apply to directly and some whom only accept applications originated through a Broker.

The question that I am often asked is, "why should I use a Broker when I can apply directly to the lender?" This is not a question that can be answered easily, and may not be a question that should be asked at all. Your emphasis, when seeking a mortgage professional, should not be on what type of entity you are applying with, but what program you are being offered; in other words, what will the services cost me and what rate I will be afforded.

There is no absolute formula for determining which route is better for you. Like so many other issues associated with home buying the answers are very fact-sensitive. Utilizing the services of a Mortgage Bank may sometimes afford you the benefit of lower rates and lower closing fees since you are applying directly to the loan provider. This is not always the case, however, since there are many instances I know of where buyers received the same deal going through a broker that they would have gotten by applying directly with the lender. In some cases lenders even provide better pricing to brokers than they do to direct customers; therefore, the customer who applied through the broker received a better rate.

The advantages of utilizing a broker are that she has the ability to shop your loan to numerous lenders as part of his service, wherein, it would be quite time consuming and costly for you to do the same thing. Additionally, if you use a competent Broker she, probably, tends to be more service oriented than a direct lender. Because she has the flexibility as to where to shop your loan, she will likely be more interested in getting to know your circumstances so that she can best utilize them to your advantage. However, sometimes there is an additional cost, or broker fee, for these services, even if the rate you receive is comparable to one you would receive from a lender. The major benefits of going to a broker are twofold:

1) If you do not have great credit a broker can find you a lender who is willing to do the loan. The broker has some leverage because he has a direct relationship with the lender.

2) Time saving-the broker will shop your application to a variety of lenders at the same time rather than the monogamous lender courtship you will have to engage in on your own.

The key to determining which program, whether offered by bank or broker, is to educate yourself on the current market circumstances. Additionally, you should ask questions. You should ask, initially, how much the services are going to cost, whether there are any up front fees, and what the current interest rates are. When quoted a rate that varies from current rate, you should find out what factors were the components, in your case, of determining that rate. It is a good idea to ask if any fees paid up front are refundable, such as application, appraisal or credit report. You should not hesitate to shop around for the best deal; however, in the world of mortgages I caution buyers, "If it seems too good to be true, it probably is."

The mortgage professional, whether affiliated with a bank or a broker, will be vital to moving the process towards a closing. He must quickly gather all of your information and make application in order to meet the time frame outlined in the Contract of Sale between the parties. He must communicate with the other real estate professionals to gather and coordinate the various services and inspections that are tied into the mortgage approval process. It is the mortgage professional who must do everything possible to ensure that you receive the amount and type of financing that will enable you to buy the home you are in contract for. In Chapter 5 of this book we will discuss the mortgage process at length. *The cost to the buyer for the services of a mortgage professional will vary depending on the type of program you are committee to and the variety of pricing options associated with each program.*

THE SELLER- The seller is the party without whom you would be unable to proceed with this particular property that you are purchasing. The seller could be an individual, a couple, an Estate, or a corporation. For your purposes, it doesn't matter who the seller is, as you will have little or no direct contact with the seller, in most cases, until the closing. In the event that the property is a FSBO, or For Sale By Owner, you may have more contact with the seller at the beginning or end of the transaction than if a Real Estate Agent had been utilized.

THE HOME INSPECTOR- The Home Inspector or Home Engineer is an individual licensed to conduct a thorough examination of the house you are prospecting for the purposes of determining its structural integrity. The inspector will have you walk through the house with him as he tests all the major systems of the house. These will include the plumbing, heating, electrical as well as the roof and appliances. A thorough inspection might take several hours and will cover many aspects of the house and its construction. The inspection is a great time to ask all of the questions about the structure and systems of the house; you will learn if the heating system is gas or oil-based, and how old the roof is. Several days after the inspection the inspector will provide you with a detailed, written report regarding findings. The report will often grade the systems from "excellent" to "poor", with numerous comments throughout. It is important that the inspection be done as early as possible in the process as the findings of the inspector may alter your plans to proceed with the purchase, or may give rise to some negotiations with the seller regarding work to be done prior to closing. It is important to read the inspector's report with a discerning eye, as he will, literally, point out every little flaw of the house that he finds. It is for you to determine which items are worth addressing, and which are just for your information. There are many people who believe that the home inspector is, for the money spent on the service, the most valuable of the players. For only several hundred dollars a good home inspector might save you several hundred thousand dollars. *The average Home Inspection ranges from $250.00 - $350.00 depending on the type of report issued and is paid by the Buyer.*

THE TERMITE INSPECTOR- The termite inspector is the individual or company that will visit the prospective property to determine the existence of any wood-destroying insect such as termites or carpenter ants. They will provide a written report on the form required by the lender and if there is damage or infestation, they will recommend treatment. *The average termite inspection runs $70.00-$90.00 and is paid by the Buyer.*

THE APPPRAISER- The appraiser is the party designated by the lender as the party to determine the value of the property you are buying. The appraiser utilizes comparable sales in the neighborhood you are buying in to determine what the value of the house is. This is not an exact science, but the results will be vital to the lender in determining the loan amount. This service offers you the protection of knowing you are not paying $500,000.00 for a house worth half that amount. *The average appraisal runs $350.00-$525.00 for a single-family residence and is paid by the Buyer.*

THE TITLE COMPANY- The title company is an entity that will not have direct contact with during the course of the transaction; however, it performs an invaluable service. The title company will prepare a report, which will provide you, the buyer, and the lender, if one exists, with certain assurances. The assurances are based upon the various searches conducted by the title companies' affiliates. The first of those assurances is that people you are in contract to buy from are the owners of the house. This may seem silly, but you would be amazed to hear the stories of people who discover the people they are in contact with are not the actual owners of the house; in fact the house isn't even for sale.

The body of the title report outlines the liens, judgments, violations, and mortgages that exist against property. This information is vital to you because if these are not addressed prior to closing they will remain encumbrances on your title: in other words, you will buy the house with those liens attached. They will become your responsibility, if not addressed, to be cleared up before you sell in years to come.

The remainder of the report highlights what the real estate taxes for the property are and which taxes are still open, what water charges are still open, and whether the seller has an open bankruptcy filing. Additionally, the survey will be attached to the report, as well as the very important Certificate of Occupancy searches. These searches, when compared to the survey will tell you if the seller has all of the legally required documents to support all of the structures at the premises. It is not uncommon to discover for the first time that an addition to a property, done by a previous owner, was undetected but is not legal. This report will put all parties on notice so that they can address the issues highlighted in the report. It may become the basis for negotiations between the parties to resolve any unforeseen issues and to get the deal closed.

The title company does more than just prepare the report: the most important function is to provide insurance that the information in the report is accurate. If it turned out that the people you bought from are not the real owners and the title company failed to discover this fact you might have recourse against them for the value of any damages incurred by you.

The cost of title insurance is set by state formula and is based upon the cost of the property and the size of any mortgage loan and is paid by the Buyer. Additional title charges, recording fees, and mortgage taxes will vary from region to region.

THE SURVEYOR- The surveyor is the party that will measure and draw the physical map, or survey of the property, in order to insure that you know exactly what you are buying in a physical sense. In other words, the surveyor will actually measure the property and structure and mark off the significant boundaries so that the actual dimensions get reduced to writing in what is called a *metes and bounds description* that will appear in the Deed of property. This survey will become part of your title report and a vital article if you choose to renovate, refinance, or sell at a later date. It will also be vital if you ever get into a boundary dispute with a neighbor whose property that "old oak tree that drops all the leaves in the fall" belongs to. *The cost of a new survey can range from $400.00-$5000.00, but if an old survey exists an inspection can take place for $75.00-$95.00 and is paid by the Buyer.*

THE INSURANCE AGENT- Your insurance agent will need to provide you with a one year prepaid policy insuring you, and the lender if there is one, against any hazards, such as fire, that would endanger the property. Under Federal Law the lender can only require that you obtain coverage for the lesser of the loan amount, or the cost to rebuild the structure. You should contact your agent to discuss the various options, costs, and policies available including liability policies in case someone gets injured at the property once you go to closing. The bank will have certain language that will be required as part of the policy, including naming them as the additional loss payee. Flood insurance may also be required, at an additional cost, if the property is in a flood zone. *The cost of insurance will vary depending on the size of the deal and the options you select.*

THE TITLE CLOSER- The title closer is the representative of the title company that will attend the closing. The closer will ensure that all taxes are paid as well as all required fees. The closer will confirm the payoff of the seller's mortgage and ensure that any checks drawn at the closing to satisfy the lien are delivered to the appropriate party. The closer will ensure that the buyer receives a "clean and clear" title. Furthermore, the title closer will provide the buyer and the bank attorney with original insurance policies for safekeeping in the event of a future question or claim. *The title closer generally receives a gratuity from the buyer ranging from $50.00 to $125.00 depending on the region.*

THE STATE AND LOCAL GOVERNMENT- I mention the state and local government because, although they will not be at the forefront of any deal, you will feel their influence throughout the transaction. Of course, the entire transaction will be conducted in accordance with the laws and regulations of the region you are in. There are very specific laws that govern real estate transactions and mortgages, ranging from licensing requirements for real estate agents to the regulations of fees that may be charged by mortgage professionals. More specifically, the seller will likely incur certain transfer taxes at the time of the sale, which are remitted to the government. Additionally, you will have to pay certain mortgage taxes if you finance your transactions. These taxes can be high as 1.75% of the mortgage amount if you are buying in one of the five boroughs of New York

City. As this is a large fee, you must be certain to calculate it into your total closing costs when preparing for your transactions.

THE UTILITY COMPANIES- The utility companies are the local, regulated businesses that provide basic services to the house you are buying. These include water, electric, gas, alarm companies, and any other companies that might provide services in the area of your new home. Your only real contact with these parties will be to notify them of a closing date and to request accounts to be opened in your name following the closing. *The costs of utility services vary from neighborhood to neighborhood.*

THE ACCOUNTANT- Your accountant may be involved to the extent that she will be invaluable to you in helping gather any necessary income documentation for a loan product that requires such documentation. It may be easier to have your mortgage professional contact your accountant directly in order to request various documents. This will save you from having to make the same request second hand, without good working knowledge of what it is you require. Additionally, your accountant will be helpful in the first year, after you buy, at determining the impact that the closing and any mortgage interest payments may have on your tax situation. *The cost of* *accounting services should be minimal to you in this transaction.*

THE SELLER'S ATTORNEY- The seller's attorney will represent the interests of the seller in proceeding with the sale of the home. The attorney will be responsible for, in most cases, preparing the Contract of Sale. Additionally, the seller's attorney will shepherd the process along for the sellers to insure that the seller's rights are protected and that the transaction proceeds in an efficient manner within the parameters of the negotiated contract. The temperament of the seller's attorney is equally as important as that of the sellers because the sellers will take significant direction from the advice of their counsel; although there is nothing you can do about this fact, it is important to keep it in mind as you proceed. There may be times when the seller's response to certain issues might be different from what you expected after meeting them. "But they seemed like such accommodating people…" is a phrase I often heard when representing buyers, and the sellers rejected their request to do such things as let the contractor start knocking down walls before the closing. This response is, probably, the product of the fact that, although, the sellers would probably love to have you start renovating their home while they still live there, their counsel probably advised them of the legal pitfalls to this approach and advised them to reject your request. Remember, as much as you and the sellers might get along, this is a business transaction. *There is no cost to the buyer for the seller's attorney.*

THE BANK ATTORNEY- The bank attorney is the host of the biggest, most sought after party in town—"YOUR CLOSING." The bank attorney will conduct the closing, which will be the first time all the principal players will be together in one place. It is her job to make certain that everything is in place, that everyone is getting along, and that everyone leaves happy. More specifically, the bank attorney must make certain that the closing is conducted in accordance with the state and local customs and that the interest of the lender is protected. It is not until the bank attorney is satisfied that all the conditions of the transaction have been met, that the title is being transferred properly, and that the lender has a valid interest in the subject property, that they will disburse the proceeds of the buyer's loan. The bank attorney is the lender's representative at the closing. Her main concern is to represent the interest of her client—the bank. She is responsible for collecting all of the conditions at the closing, such as contracts, deeds, and copies of certified checks. *The cost of the* *bank's attorney ranges from $450-$850, and is paid by the buyer in most cases.*

THE BUYER'S ATTORNEY- The buyer's attorney, in my opinion, is the most critical player in the entire cast of characters associated with this transaction. Although a buyer could certainly undertake to represent himself in a purchase, I cannot imagine why anyone would want to. Despite the fact that representing buyers, sellers, and banks is what I did for a living, I retained the services of counsel for the purchase of my home. Why? Because you should have a professional insulate you from direct contact with numerous professionals and lay people associated with the transaction. Remember, again, that this is a business transaction, and having the benefit of the advice of an objective professional is invaluable. It is dangerous to play counsel and client when hundreds of thousands of dollars are on the line.

The buyer's attorney performs the tasks that make him the veritable ringleader for this circus prior to closing. It is the role of the buyer's attorney to work with every single one of the professionals outlined here and coordinate their efforts in a productive, efficient manner. It is the role of the competent buyer's attorney to keep the lines of communication open between all parties and to make sure that all of the various deadlines are being met by the parties to ensure a smooth transaction. It is also the role of the buyer's attorney to act as your voice of reason. This is not to say that your attorney should make any decisions for you; after all, it is not his house that is being bought, nor is it his money being utilized. However, the attorney should inform you of all the implications of the variety of choices you will face along the way so that you can make the most informed decision. Finally, the buyer's attorney should be there to assist you in the event that you get into any trouble along the way. If you get denied a mortgage, or if the sellers decide to back out on the eve of the closing, you want to know that you have a competent professional to assist you and advise you. *The average cost of a buyer's attorney ranges from $500.00 to $1,000.00, depending on the size of the transaction, the region, and the services provided.*

It is the work of all these players to keep the real estate machine moving forward in this country. With the number of individuals associated with every transaction it is sometimes amazing that any deals ever get closed. For the most part everyone performs his task professionally and in a timely manner and, as a result, the transaction does progress like a well-oiled machine. However, there are times that one or more problems do arise, either revealed by one of these professionals, or sometimes even caused by them. These problems will not necessarily be the unraveling of the entire transaction and your life's dream; they will just be obstacles to overcome in getting to your final goal: **home ownership**.

One final note: although I tried to give a range of prices for the services rendered by the various professionals, it is hard to pinpoint exactly what the costs associated with the transaction will be without specific facts associated with you and the houses you are buying. In general, a guide that has always worked well is that the total closing costs, generally, range from 5%-8% of the total purchase price. If you estimate conservatively at 6.5% of the total purchase price as a starting place, I believe you won't go wrong.

The Players
Contact list

Property Address:_____

Real Estate Agent:
Name:_____
Phone:_____
Email:_____

Your Lawyer:
Name:_____
Phone:_____
Email:_____

Termite Inspector:
Name:_____
Phone:_____
Email:_____

Title Company:
Name:_____
Phone:_____
Email:_____

Insurance Agent:
Name:_____
Phone:_____
Email:_____

Mortgage Broker/Banker:
Name:_____
Phone:_____
Email:_____

Home Inspector:
Name:_____
Phone:_____
Email:_____

Appraisal Company:
Name:_____
Phone:_____
Email:_____

Bank Attorney:
Name:_____
Phone:_____
Email:_____

The Surveyor:
Name:_____
Phone:_____
Email:_____

Chapter Notes

Chapter 4: Choosing the Right Lawyer

In the prior chapter I expressed the significance of the buyer's attorney in the process of buying your home. The choice of whom you are going to retain to fulfill this role is among the most important you will make in this process. Making a wrong decision, while probably not fatal, can significantly alter the dynamics of the entire transaction. Just about any lawyer you know has done a house closing at one time or another during his career. Property is one of the fundamental components in the curriculum of any law school. Most lawyers have some working knowledge of real estate. In fact, I would go so far as to say that I would be surprised to find any attorney that didn't have the skills to get you through a home purchase; after all, it is not brain surgery. The question you must ask yourself is, "Do I just want to get through this purchase?" or do you want it to be as trouble-free as possible?

The point I am trying to make is that I believe that with something as critical as buying your home you should rely on a lawyer who deals primarily in real estate matters. Lawyers, unlike doctors, do not have specialty degrees. What makes a lawyer a real estate lawyer as opposed to a personal injury lawyer is not the product of different academic degrees but the product of the area of practice that the lawyer has devoted himself to. Regardless of the fact that the personal injury lawyer and the real estate lawyer might have the same academic degree, I personally would not rely on one to perform the services attributed to the other. I believe, although an extreme example, it would be the equivalent of going to an eye surgeon to set a broken arm. While I'm sure that the eye surgeon, having gone to medical school, is minimally qualified to perform the task. I would pass on his or her services, if possible, in favor of an orthopedist.

Real estate, like any area of specialty, has a language all of its own, with its own subtle nuances. There are numerous pitfalls associated with every real estate transaction that are unique to real estate matters. The real estate community is a small, tight knit group. Most of the professionals know each other and have a familiarity of the styles associated with other key players in the community. The one thread that strings together the members of this community is the desire to get the deal done even if it means shifting gears along the way and compromising. For most people, whether they are buyers, sellers, or real estate professionals, the possibility of litigation is only a last resort in any real estate transaction. It is a poor symbol of a complete failure of the parties to put the desire to meet their respective goals of buying and selling ahead of their disagreements. Therefore, it is essential that the most professional, competent, and experienced team be assembled to guide you through the process, starting with your lawyer.

All of these factors make it essential that the lawyer retained to represent you in buying a home be fully familiar with the implications associated with the process. Furthermore, that the lawyer must be of the temperament to understand the respective goals of the parties. There is nothing worse, in my opinion, than a lawyer being an impediment to getting the deal "closed."

When seeking out a lawyer you should seek a lawyer who concentrates on real estate matters. You can look on the Internet, call your local Bar Association referral service, or utilize a personal reference from someone whose opinion you respect. I would suggest that, if possible, you start out by speaking with a lawyer that came to you by recommendation from an individual who utilized his or her services for a prior real estate transaction. This is the best way to find someone who not only concentrates in the area of real estate, but someone who has a track record.

Many people will ask me if it's okay to utilize the services of a lawyer that was referred to them by their real estate agent. I understand that some people naturally suspect that this lawyer may not be prepared to serve their interests, but may be beholden to the real estate agent. This is not necessarily true. Any competent lawyer I know, while having a good relationship with a real estate agent, honors his duty to represent his client honestly and zealously. You should simply utilize the same criteria in interviewing the real estate agent's referral as you would any other professional candidate.

You should ask the lawyer you are considering what percentage of his practice is devoted to real estate matters. Although there is no number that is the key, I would suggest retaining a lawyer who devotes at least 65% of his practice to real estate matters. You want to know that the lawyer you select is fully familiar with real estate matters, their nuances, and will have the time to devote to your purchase.

You should ask the lawyer you are prospecting if there are other professionals in the office who you can speak with if he is unavailable. This is important. Nothing is more frustrating than calling to discuss your matter to discover that the lawyer is in court for the next several days and that there is no one else in the firm familiar with your matter. This is not only frustrating, but due to lack of counsel, can cause you to make a detrimental decision regarding your purchase.

When prospecting a lawyer, and discussing the nature of law practice, keep in mind that faced with the prospect of balancing time devoted to a $1 million dollar lawsuit against the time spent on a real estate purchase, it is natural to expect that a lawyer may focus his efforts on a big pay day lawsuit. When you deal with a real estate lawyer, there is no conflict. All of that lawyer's time is spent on real estate matters, and the way a real estate lawyer builds his practice is through referrals from other satisfied real estate clients. The key factor is that prior clients were satisfied with the way their transaction was handled.

You should also discuss fees with your prospective lawyer. Although I do not believe that fees alone should be the determining factor in choosing your lawyer, I do believe it is important to know what you are paying for. In the booming 1980s, most lawyers charged 1% of the purchase price as a minimum fee. Fees today are calculated on a more competitive, flat fee rate; however, you should inquire as to what services are included in that fee. You should stay away from lawyers who bill hourly and for phone calls on a residential real estate matter, not because they are doing anything improper, but simply a fact of transaction, it is vital that the lawyer and client speak often regarding the progress of the transaction. If a client is deterred from calling due to the fear of getting an excessive bill, he may withhold vital information that could significantly alter the outcome of the transaction. Most good real estate lawyers will charge a reasonable rate and will provide a variety of services. Don't make the mistake of simply price shopping for a lawyer when buying a house. Saving money by going with a lawyer you are less than comfortable with is not saving money at all. In your evaluation of the services provided by a competent real estate lawyer, the professional's legal fee is the best money spent on your new home purchase.

Finally, you should utilize your instincts in selecting a lawyer regardless of what his credentials are. You should be comfortable with the lawyer and feel that she is approachable and professional in demeanor. Remember, this individual will be interacting with several dozen other professionals on your file. As in any other business, your lawyer must be able to communicate in a way that results in the most benefit for you in proceeding with your purchase. If you don't feel comfortable with your lawyer no one else probably will either and, although he may understand his duties, he may not, in actuality, be the right choice.

Chapter Notes

Chapter 5:   The Mortgage

The dream of homeownership is made possible for the vast majority of Americans only with the help of financing from third parties. Very few Americans would be able to save enough money on their own to acquire a property, or have relatives benevolent enough to gift them the amount required to obtain property.

The advent of mortgage financing, together with its support from the federal and state governments, has made the dream of home ownership a reality for the average, hard working American citizen. In the 1990s, the broadening of the non-conventional financing products, including those referred to as "sub-prime" products even extended the promise of home ownership to those individuals who were hard-working with good incomes, but had less than perfect credit. This approach to financing incorporated the most personal methodology in assessing individual situations on a case-by-case basis within certain flexible parameters as opposed to simply qualifying individuals on "numbers" alone, with no humanistic approach.

Although we have discussed various aspects of the mortgage process throughout the book, this chapter will focus on some of the "nuts and bolts" so that you will be able to keep track of the process as it is occurring.

The mortgage process is based on the premise that a lender will extend financing to you after assessing your ability to repay, based upon retaining an interest in your property as collateral. Depending on the state you live in the security interest may come in different forms. In New York you are the owner of the house and the lender obtains a lien against your property. In other states the lender will hold your house "in trust" until such time as you satisfy their loan. In either case the consequences of a failure to pay your mortgage payments for a protracted period of time will result in your losing that property in a legal proceeding known as foreclosure.

There are a wide variety of mortgage products to choose from. Most mortgages utilize what are called Fannie Mae/Freddie Mac guidelines, which are simply underwriting guidelines established by the Federal government in determining your eligibility for these products; (i.e. your debt to income ratio, etc.). There are also federally insured products, like FHA loans, which allow for smaller down payments and, sometimes, less rigid credit requirements. There are also VA loans for Veterans who qualify, which are similar to FHA loans, but will allow purchasers to put no money down on the signing of the contract of sale. Many states offer their own programs for first time homebuyers within a certain income bracket like New York's widely popular SONY MAE program. Finally, there are the non-conventional "sub-prime" programs, which are more flexible in underwriting guidelines, but are sometimes more costly than their alternatives.

Whether your initial contact with a mortgage professional is prior to prospecting, as advised, or after you go to contract, your first phase will be the intake process. This is the process of gathering all of the information regarding you and your prospective property, including your name, social security number, your employment, your credit history, the property address, the purchase price, the amount you have saved in assets, and much more, depending on the professional you are speaking with. In today's market many individuals submit this information through a number of Internet-based online mortgage services. These services are simply adjunct devices for mortgage professionals, such as banks and brokers, to reach out to a growing sector of the population. They offer no more, nor less, than the mortgage professional who has set up the website. Your individual inclinations regarding any Internet service will determine whether you are comfortable with this method of applying; whether you would prefer to speak with a live person or prefer a relationship with your computer. Many buyers still have concerns about security and privacy issues related to an online application and, in my opinion, most buyers would still prefer to speak to a human being regarding their personal information and finances.

After all of your information has been gathered your mortgage professional will run your credit, perform his analysis, and prepare an approval or conditional commitment. These commitments are usually based upon a number of conditions being met, some by the borrower, himself, and some by other real estate professionals, like the appraiser. In the case of broker originated applications the broker will shop your application to several banks in order to get you the best deal possible with the least amount of conditions required.

The approval that you will receive will have a prospective loan amount and a proposed interest rate. Hopefully, these terms will meet what you need in order to complete the purchase of your home. If they do not, you will need to speak to your mortgage professional about what may be done to possibly meet those needs.

You will be faced with a number of choices at every turn; whether to lock in an interest rate or to float it, whether to go with a fixed rate mortgage or an adjustable rate mortgage, whether to pay points or not pay points. Again, there is no right or wrong answer to these questions. The answer must be the result of analysis of your personal situation and needs.

The interest rate question is complex and is more related to timing than anything else. In a market where interest rates are declining there is no rush to lock in a rate; it is probably better to take a wait and see approach. Once rates seem to level off, or start to climb, you could lock in the rate. In a market where interest rates are climbing there is an inclination to want to lock in the rate as early as possible.

The question of how long to lock the rate in for is one that is troublesome. If you lock it in for a short period of time you will get the best rate available; however, if you don't close within the lock-in time you will face additional fees and the possibility of being assessed the prevailing, or higher, rate at the date of your re-lock. The question you need to ask, and this is where your lawyer plays a vital role, is "how close to closing this deal am I"? If the answer is "four months," you had better not lock in the rate for thirty days. Your lawyer will have to communicate with the seller's lawyer, and within the parameters of the contract of sale, determine if the deal is progressing according to the schedule originally contemplated. These factors of unpredictability, which will make it impossible to nail down the date with exact certainty; however, by your lawyer communicating effectively with the seller's lawyer, you will be able to narrow the margin for error in selecting a lock-in period.

The adjustable versus fixed rate question is also complex. While most people like the certainty of a fixed rate it may be wise at times to select an adjustable rate. When interest rates are very high you can always get a better rate with an adjustable program. This will buy you time until the rates come down and you can refinance for a lower, fixed rate. Similarly, if you are advancing in your career and cleaning up your credit you may be wise to start with a lower rate, adjustable mortgage to keep your payments down initially. Once you move up the corporate ladder and clean up your credit you can refinance for the lower fixed rate you are now eligible for. This is a personal decision that will rely on extensive talks with your spouse, your lawyer, and your mortgage professional.

The issue of points is one of the most confusing of the mortgage process. All of the major ads for mortgages entice you with their "no points" slogan. The premise is that points are bad and you shouldn't have to pay them. This is not an absolute and the question of whether or not to pay points should be explored carefully. The issue that this question relates most closely to is how much you have saved for the purchase of your house versus how much you can afford to pay on a monthly basis. In other words, there are times when it makes sense to pay points on a mortgage to "buy down" your rate. This will have the effect of lowering your interest rate and your monthly payment.

A point is defined as "one percent of the loan amount." So, if you are borrowing $150,000.00 for the purchase of your home then a point is the equivalent of $1,500. When faced with this choice you must analyze what you are getting for this point. In other words, if it would cost you one point on the previously mentioned loan amount to lower your interest rate from 8% to 6.5% it might be worth it, whereas, if the same point only lowered your rate from 8% to 7.75% it might not be worth it. Even in the first example, if you valued saving money on closing costs, because of a limited budget, more than lowering the cost of your monthly payment, you would be more likely to pass on the idea of paying points no matter how much benefit you received from them. When I bought my house I hadn't saved a tremendous amount of money but my income was improving every year. I was more concerned about keeping my closing costs low than I was about keeping my mortgage payment low so I opted to close at a slightly higher interest rate paying no points.

Along with contemplating all of these choices you will be responsible for gathering the documentation for your mortgage professional as dictated by the bank's underwriter. The underwriter is the party at the bank that establishes the conditions necessary to issue a mortgage commitment in each applicant's case and the individual who determines when those conditions have been satisfied so that the loan may be set to close. These conditions may vary slightly from bank to bank and from program to program. They may include such items as presenting two (2) recent pay stubs for review, presenting twelve (12) months worth of bank statements, explaining any bad credit by letter, and approving the appraisal of the property.

The loan processor, whether the bank's or the broker's, will be the party that you communicate with in the collection of these stipulations or conditions. The processor will hound you daily if you haven't met his deadlines, and will also assist you in finding alternate material for the underwriter's approval in the event that you are having trouble gathering the documentation required.

At some point early in the application process, you will receive from your mortgage professional a **Good Faith Estimate of Closing Costs**. This is a document required to be issued by the Federal government, and represents exactly what its name suggests. It is designed to help you understand how much the mortgage you are applying for will cost you and how much you will need to close your loan. It is important that you review this document carefully with your mortgage professional and your lawyer. Any questions that you have regarding the fees associated with this loan should be asked now, and not at the closing table on the day of closing. You should fully understand what your costs are and what they represent. As indicated earlier, each program may vary in its closing costs; the important thing is to understand what you are paying for and to be certain it is what you were promised and what you bargained for.

Although accurate on bank and broker fees, the **Good Faith Estimate** should not be relied on to reveal all of your costs; hence its characterization as an estimate. You should review the document with your lawyer to discuss how much the title charges will be, how much his or her fee will be, any escrows for taxes and insurance, and other miscellaneous fees attributed with the deal. In this way you will be fully prepared, financially, to close the deal, and won't be embarrassed at the closing table by coming up a little short.

Once the appraisal has been approved, the mortgage choices have been selected, and all the conditions have been met, your loan will be cleared to close. It is at this point that your loan will be sent to the bank attorney for legal review of the title report and the scheduling of a closing title.

There are occasions when once the borrower commences the mortgage process he will be declined as an applicant. If you are the borrower your response to this scenario is critical to the transaction and to your financial security. It is important, as stressed throughout this book, to make your application as early as possible. This will tell you early on whether you qualify for a mortgage or not. As we talked about previously, if you do not, you will need to deal with that reality. More likely, if you were pre-qualified, you will qualify and go into contract. However, something along the way may cause you to be denied, such as a change in circumstances, or a discovery of some unforeseen impediment to proceeding with the approval process.

In today's mortgage market you may discover that a denial along the way may be a stumbling block to getting to your goal but not, necessarily, a fatal determination. Especially if you are utilizing a broker, your broker can shop the loan to another bank, or request that the denial be re-evaluated by a senior underwriter. Perhaps the denial was based on some misinformation and a correction will alter the outcome in your favor. An example of this type of misinformation that comes to mind might be that a third party with a similar name to yours has several judgments against them. The bank's credit report may confuse the two named individuals and your denial may be based on someone else's bad credit. Once you intervene and prove that those credit items are not yours you might be approved for the mortgage. The point is that an aggressive approach is essential to preserving your deal and keeping your mortgage approval process moving forward.

There will be unfortunate cases when the denial will be fatal; when no matter what is said or done, a mortgage will not be obtained. These cases demand immediate intervention by your lawyer to ensure that the deal is canceled in a legal and timely manner and that your down payment is returned. A failure to cooperate with the mortgage bank as a reason for denial, or a failure to notify the seller's lawyer in a timely manner of the denial, may result in your being in default of the contract of sale and forfeiting your down payment. Nothing adds insult to injury more than not only losing your chance to buy the house of your dreams, but also losing your hard earned down payment of as much as 10% of the purchase price.

This chapter only summarizes the mortgage process. It is the heart of most real estate purchases. It is a process that is detail-oriented, labor intensive, and costly. A majority of the key players in the real estate transaction will revolve around the issuance of the mortgage commitment. Without mortgage financing most deals simply would not happen. Many people do not understand why the process is so complicated. I always advise my prospective buyers not to make the mistake of looking at the mortgage financier as a big, multi-million dollar entity with money to spare. I ask them instead to pretend for a moment that they are in the position of a mortgage bank. A person that you have never met before comes to you and asks to borrow $500,000.00 to buy a house that you have never seen, will never own, and will never live in. Wouldn't you want to do everything you could to gather as much information about the person and the property in order to minimize the chances that you would lose your investment?

Of course you would!

Shortly after you make a mortgage application, you should receive the following documents:

1. **A Good Faith Estimate of Closing Costs—** This document will help you, generally, identify your closing costs and prepare yourself for the eventual closing of your purchase.

2. **A Truth In Lending Form—** This form identifies some of the features of your loan, including whether or not not there will be a payment penalty and how much the loan will cost you over its entire term if never prepaid.

These forms should be discussed with your mortgage professional and reviewed by your real estate attorney.

Definition of Truth-in-Lending Terms

Annual Percentage Rate

This is not the Note rate for which the borrower applied. The Annual Percentage Rate (APR) is the cost of the loan in percentage terms, taking into account various loan charges of which interest is only one. Other charges that are used in calculation of the APR are Private Mortgage Insurance or FHA Mortgage Premium (where applicable) and Prepaid finance charges (loan discount, origination fees, prepaid interest, and other credit costs.) The APR is calculated by spreading these charges over the life of the loan that results in a rate higher than the interest rate shown on your Mortgage/Deed of Trust Note. If interest were the only Finance Charge, then the interest rate and the APR would be the same.

Prepaid Finance Charges

Prepaid Finance Charges are certain charges made in connection with the loan and which must be paid upon the close of the loan. The Federal Reserve Board in Regulation Z defines these charges and the charges must be paid by the borrower. Non-origination fee, "Points" or Discount, Private Mortgage Insurance or FHA Mortgage Insurance, excluded from the Prepaid Finance Charges such as appraisal fees and credit report fees.

Finance Charge

The amount of interest, prepaid finance charge and certain insurance premiums (if any) which the borrower will be expected to pay over the life of the loan.

Amount Financed

The loan amount applied for less than the prepaid finance charges. Prepaid finance charges can be found on the Good Faith Estimate/Settlement Statement (HUD-1 or 1A). For example, if the borrower's note is for $100,000 and the Prepaid Finance Charges total $5,000 the Amount Financed would be $95,000. The Amount Financed is the figure on which the Annual Percentage Rate is based.

Total of Payments

This figure represents the total of all payments made toward principal, interest, and mortgage insurance (if applicable) over the life of the loan.

Payment Schedule

The dollar figures in the Payment Schedule represent (if applicable) over the life of the loan. These figures will not reflect taxes and insurance or any temporary buy down payments contributed by the seller.

Chapter 6:   The Process

Throughout the previous chapters of this book I have discussed various aspects of the home buying process. However, at the inception I told you that it was my intent to guide you through the whole process. Now that you have familiarity with some of the key concepts and obstacles associated with the process I can walk you through the process. I am going to guide you through the process from the time you find the house of your dreams until you go to closing. I will utilize an amalgam of circumstances I gathered from my years of experience in handling real estate matters, when I was a licensed attorney practicing in New York, and provide you with a chronological tour of the transaction. Not every one of you will find that the process unfolds in exactly this way; however, it a realistic outline.

Friday, May 1, 2015 – You and your wife, after months of seeing houses, find one that seems to be exactly what you were looking for. It is in the school district where you want your kids to go to school, in your price range, and meets all physical and cosmetic specifications you are looking for.
You inform the real estate agent of the price you are willing to offer. She speaks with the listing agent and informs you that your offer has been accepted.

She then asks you for the name of your lawyer for the binder. You provide her with the name of a lawyer you are considering using after having spoken to him on previous occasions.

The agent will then ask you if you are planning to have and engineer examine the premises. There will be subtle pressure not to have an engineer or home inspector look at the property for fear that what the engineer finds will raise issues that will cause you to change your mind, or begin negotiations regarding conditions. I would argue that this is the precise reason you should have an engineer, and encourage you to resist any pressure to the contrary. Additionally, should you decline an inspection, you will be waiving your right to have your home inspected at a later date; even if you were to hire an engineer later on in the process to inspect the premises it would not affect the price of your home in any way.

The agent will then ask you to sign a binder, which outlines the terms of the deal, and to offer a minimal deposit to hold the house. This sum is deminimus, and may be as little as $100.00. Many buyers fear signing the binder without an attorney's review. It is perfectly acceptable to sign the binder if it correctly states the terms of the deal AND has a clause to make the binder and the deal subject to your attorney's review and approval. You sign the binder.

You have now taken the first official step towards buying your home.

Saturday, May 2, 2015 – You speak to several lawyers, and decide on the one who you would like to represent you in the transaction. The lawyer, either on the telephone or in person, will conduct an intake requesting as much information about the deal, the property, and the players who have appeared so far as you can provide. At this stage you may not be able to provide too much detail about the transaction. One of the best and easiest ways to provide your lawyer with key information on the deal is to provide him with a copy of the binder and real estate agent's information. Once your lawyer has the real estate agent's information he will be able to fill in any missing gaps and ask any questions from one real estate professional to another.

Your lawyer will also, in all likelihood, encourage you to conduct an engineer's inspection if you weren't already planning to do one. He will ask that a copy of the report be provided to him for his review. Additionally, in the event that you are unfamiliar with the name of a competent engineer, your lawyer can provide you with a list of names of qualified candidates. This brings to light the importance of good real estate counsel. Your lawyer will always be able to provide you with an extensive list of competent real estate professionals to choose from as the deal progresses.

Monday, May 4, 2015 – You meet the engineer at the house to do the inspection. The engineer takes you through a one-hour tour of the house, performing her various tests and analysis on the structure and the appliances. The whole time the engineer is educating you on the specifics of this house from the appliances to the roof to the heating system. Along the way the engineer will ask some questions of the homeowner, or of the broker, about the house, and will point out certain trouble areas. Before departing the engineer will provide you with a verbal overview of the house and a succinct verbal summarization of her results. She will not tell you whether or not to buy the house. That is a decision that only you can make. She will simply point out trouble areas for your consideration.

You should remind the engineer of the time pressure you are under and ask the engineer to forward a copy of the report to your lawyer as soon as possible.

Tuesday, May 5, 2015 – The verbal report has been favorable, although certain issues are raised. You call your lawyer to tell him what you have learned and tell him to look out for the hard copy of the engineer's report.

It is at this point that your lawyer will reach out to the seller's lawyer. He will inform the seller's lawyer that the engineer's report has been done and that it warrants the contracts being prepared and forwarded to your lawyer for review and signature. Some basic discussion of the terms will ensue, but nothing major until the contracts are before both parties and lawyers.

Wednesday, May 6, 2015 – Your lawyer receives the hard copy of the engineer's report. Careful review discloses that there are no major issues to be addressed, except for some leaking plumbing pipes in an auxiliary bathroom and a broken burner on the electric stovetop in the kitchen.

Saturday, May 9, 2015 – Your lawyer receives the proposed Contract of Sale from the seller's lawyer. He reviews them for accuracy of terms, based upon the binder. He also goes through his standard review of the contract addressing any of the legal issues he feels may exist. Every real estate lawyer has his own checklist of items that he requires when reviewing a proposed Contract of Sale. This checklist, whether implicit or explicit, will become the basis for changes to a proposed contract that does not meet all the expectations of your lawyer.

Monday, May 11, 2015 – You visit your lawyer to review the Contract of Sale. Your lawyer addresses all of the key terms and conditions of the contract to insure that you both understand the terms of the contract and that the terms are what you agreed to when you made your offer on the house. The issues raised in the engineer's report will be incorporated into the contract at this time. This is the best time to ask any questions that are on your mind and to bring up any terms that were discussed by you and the real estate agent, but are not in the contract. For the most part, if it does not appear in writing in the contract, regardless of what was promised orally, it will not become part of the deal. So speak now, or forever hold your peace.

Once the terms are discussed, and agreed upon, you will sign several copies of the Contract of Sale; generally, one for each lawyer and two extras for the buyers and sellers. You will also write a personal check representing the contract down payment. In New York, that down payment is made payable to the order of the seller's lawyer to be held in a segregated, or escrow account, until closing.

Tuesday, May 12, 2015 –Your lawyer will likely receive a phone call from the seller's lawyer to discuss the proposed changes to the Contract of Sale. On the issues of legal contention, the lawyers will likely come to some agreement between themselves. On the issues relating to the substantive underlying terms the lawyers will merely mirror their clients' positions within the parameters of the negotiating room afforded each of them. In your case the sellers agree to repair the plumbing leaks, but not to repair the stovetop. For the broken appliance, they agree to give you a $50.00 credit at the closing. Your lawyer will note the new proposal, or counter-offer, and advise the seller's lawyer that he (your lawyer) will need to speak with you first.

The decision on whether to accept the credit is not a legal one. It is a decision that you, as the buyer, can make on your own. You can ask your lawyer's opinion, but it has no value more or less than asking any non-lawyer. Assuming you decide to take the credit, let your lawyer know so that he may convey the same to the seller's lawyer.

Wednesday, May 13, 2015—Your lawyer informs the seller's lawyer that there is the basis of a deal that we will be expecting the fully executed contracts back shortly.

Saturday, May 16, 2015—Your lawyer receives the fully executed contract and reviews them for any new alterations. In the event that they are acceptable, your lawyer will now do two important things:

1)   Order a termite inspection of the property, and

2)   Order an abstract of title for the property.

A real estate lawyer will order these searches early to insure that the timelines of the Contract of Sale are met and that any problems are uncovered early enough in the process to cure them.

Sunday, May 17, 2015—You will need to get your fully executed Contract of Sale to your mortgage professional to "get the ball rolling" on the mortgage process. Again, time is an essential factor of this process. You want to discover as early as possible if there will be any problems with your financing. Be certain to provide your mortgage professional with your lawyer's information. Encourage your mortgage professional to communicate with your lawyer on any matter in question. Do not make the mistake of being concerned that your lawyer will not want to be bothered dealing with someone other than you; remember, a competent real estate lawyer will expect and welcome these calls. Communication is key to helping you buy your home.

At this time, you will receive a **Good Faith Estimate**, **Loan Application**, and a **Truth In**

Lending Form if you haven't received them previously. Review them for accuracy, ask any questions regarding them, and be sure to get a set of copies to your lawyer for his review.

Monday, May 18, 2015—The termite inspection is sent to your lawyer and reveals some termite damage and a small amount of infestation near a sill plate in the basement. Your lawyer must immediately put the seller's lawyer on notice that the condition exists and request treatment, repair, and a one-year guarantee from a termite company. The seller could choose to cancel the deal at this point and refund your money; however, if termites do exist, the seller will have to treat them in order to sell the house to anyone. The seller is not obligated to utilize your company. He may choose his own company so long as the company is licensed and performs the proper work and treatment.

Wednesday, May 20, 2015—An appraisal for the property is conducted. Although you attend the appraisal you may not know on the spot what the exact appraised value of the house is. The appraiser will prepare a written report, with photographs, and send it to your mortgage professional for his review.

Monday, May 25 2015—The appraisal for your purchase is delivered to your mortgage professional's office. It meets the value necessary to proceed with the transaction, and the bank accepts its value. This is a major milestone in the transaction, especially in the market where values are increasing rapidly, as they did in the late 1990's. Appraisers derive their values from sales of recent homes in the neighborhood you are purchasing. They use "comps" or houses of comparable style in the neighborhood to assess value. In a market where the demand for houses exceeds supply and buyers often get into bidding wars, driving up the sales prices daily, the appraised values may lag behind until many of the sales are recorded. Therefore, if you are buying the most expensive house in the neighborhood, the appraiser may deliver a report that indicates that the house you are buying is not worth the price you are paying. This determination is not, necessarily, fatal. It can be dealt with through further analysis of recent local home sales. In the worst-case scenario, your lawyer could negotiate a reduction of the sales price to meet the appraised value.

Tuesday, May 26, 2015—The lawyers for the parties receive the preliminary title search report.

Wednesday, May 27, 2015—Your lawyer reviews the preliminary search and finds no major outstanding title objections. Any of the objections that your lawyer feels are pertinent will be conveyed to the seller's lawyer by written correspondence. The seller's lawyer must address these title issues prior to any closing on the property. Title objections are a major cause of delay in home buying. Many lawyers make the mistake of not ordering and reviewing the title search early enough in the process to be beneficial. Therefore, when problems are discovered it is too close to the closing date to effectively deal with them without causing a major inconvenience to the parties.

Friday, May 29, 2015—The seller's lawyer presents your lawyer an old survey of the property, which was in the possession of the sellers. This will save you from having to purchase a new one, as surveys are required on most purchases. Instead, a survey inspector from the title company will visit the property with the survey, note any changes from the survey date, and file a report outlining the changes. This inspection, in comparison to the cost of a new survey, is relatively inexpensive. The survey inspection of the property you are buying revealed no major structural changes to the house or the property line. This is significant because many buyers learn for the first time when they see the survey that "the old tree that I fell in love with" isn't on their property at all. In most cases these are not the issues that make or break deals, but they are important to know and are required by the lender for title insurance purposes.

May-June, 2015—You have spent the whole month in gathering and delivering documentation to the loan processor assigned to your deal. This contact, as mentioned previously, will be continuous and it will seem that every time you think you have provided the last document another gets added to the list. There is not much you can do about this since underwriting is an ongoing process, and resisting the process will only result in delays. Remember to put yourself in the shoes of the lender and you may realize the pursuit of all these conditions is not for the sole purpose of irritating you.

Friday, June 5, 2015—The title company's *Certificate of Occupancy* search reveals that the property is a legal one family dwelling with a garage; which is also what the survey shows and reflects what you, physically, observed when you prospected the house. This search is also vital to proceeding. Sellers often discover that there are missing certificates or open permits once the title report is received. As a buyer you will be hard pressed to find a lender who will finance your deal without the house having all of its certificates in place. You will be equally hard pressed to find a lawyer who would let you proceed to a closing without such certificates. Keep in mind that although this house is wonderful you may wish to sell it some day. At that time you will incur great cost and cause great delays if you have to first apply to legalize your home. If certificate issues arise the seller will not be happy about them; however, he will not be able to sell the house, in most cases, without correcting the problem and legalizing the structure.

Monday, June 8, 2015—You receive your mortgage commitment from the bank. Congratulations! This is an important step towards home ownership. The commitment may have some minor conditions but any major stumbling blocks should be overcome by now. This commitment represents the formalization of a financial institution's desire to lend you the money to buy your home.

The commitment will identify the bank attorney and make the closing of title subject to some standard conditions, including review of title by the bank attorney.

The commitment is also important for you in that it solidifies the deal for you as buyer. After you receive a commitment, if the deal is cancelled due to no fault of the seller, you stand the chance to lose your down payment. That is why it is so important to make sure that as much work is done as early in the process as possible so that once the commitment is issued, closing is, virtually, a formality.

It is customary at the time a commitment is issued to pay a fee to your mortgage professional. Some call this fee the "commitment fee", others the "lock-in fee" (to lock in the rate). The amount that you pay at this time will be credited at closing to your total closing costs. However, if you don't close, the fee is non-refundable. There are very few lenders that do not require some fees to be paid upon the issuance of a commitment.

Wednesday, June 10, 2015—Your lawyer forwards the title search to the bank attorney and a copy of the commitment to the seller's lawyer. Serious discussions will now commence regarding the settlement of a closing date. The buyers and the sellers will have to seriously examine their calendars to try to coordinate their respective moves. If the seller is also buying another house it is important for you lawyer to get a handle on whether that transaction is moving forward according to schedule, or whether that second transaction will delay your purchase. This is an important question that must be answered with some certainty. Long delays in the seller's ultimate purchase may cause you to delay your purchase, and may result in great financial hardship to you by losing your low, locked-in interest rate, or your mortgage commitment, entirely. Once again, you will need to know early on if a problem exists so that it may be dealt with.

Monday, June 15, 2015—You should start shopping around for homeowner's insurance for the property. The commitment will outline minimum requirements for insurance, but you should speak with your agent and lawyer regarding meeting your personal needs. I always point out the buyer that did not heed my warning about securing adequate and timely insurance. She called her lawyer weeks after the closing, in a panic, because a visitor had taken a terrible fall in her home and she was not covered in the event of a lawsuit for his injuries.

You will, in all likelihood, need to bind one full year of coverage, commencing on the closing date, and lasting for one year. The original documentation will need to be presented at the closing.

Tuesday, June 23, 2015—The bank attorney reviews the file and the title and marks the file "clear to close." It is now, if all the parties can coordinate their schedules, that a closing date can be set.

The three lawyers will have to speak to each other to coordinate their busy schedules with that of their clients'. Despite the tremendous difficulty in coordinating the schedules of at least six individuals, it happens everyday and will happen in you case.

Tuesday, June 30, 2015—After some discussion, a mutually agreeable date is selected and booked with the bank attorney. Your lawyer's assistant sends out a confirming letter to all parties, including the title company and the real estate agents, all of whom will be attending the closing.

Your lawyer will give you a list of last minute things to do to get ready for the big day. These tasks are tedious, but are imperative to a smooth transaction.

You call the phone company, the water company, the electric company, and the cable company to inform them of your move. In most areas these services will have new accounts opened in your name, starting after the close date. A final reading of the seller's charges will be taken prior to closing and the bills forwarded to the sellers at their new address.

Thursday, July 2, 2015—You will set up with the real estate agent a final "walk-through" of the house. The purpose of this visit is to check on the current status of the house. It is designed to help you determine that the house is in the same condition as when you saw it and placed your offer. This is not the time to re-evaluate your decision and look for reasons to re-negotiate the purchase price. Nor is it the time to comment on items that existed at the time you saw your house, but were never previously raised. What you are looking to confirm is that the house is in the same condition as when you saw it, not better. I heard the tale of one buyer who asked if he could do the engineer's report that he had refused at the commencement of the transaction during the "walk-through". The answer to that question is "No". It is not appropriate, or timely, to conduct the engineer's report at this point. If you failed to conduct an engineer's report at the appropriate time, you waive your right to ever do so and have it impact the transaction.

In the event there are issues that need to be addressed regarding the condition of the premises, don't panic. You should point the issues and items out to the agent and call your lawyer. If the items are major a postponement of the closing may be necessary. However, in most cases the list will serve as the basis for a small negotiation, and possible adjustment, at the closing.

Saturday, July 11, 2015—In the several days prior to the closing your lawyer will obtain the actual closing costs associated with the deal. He will prepare an itemization of those costs and help you determine how much money you need to close. You will be instructed as to how your checks should be payable, and what types of checks are acceptable (i.e. certified or teller's check as opposed to personal check). Your lawyer should be able to calculate these figures and explain them to you with relative ease. If the figures don't make sense to you, be sure to say so and go over them with your lawyer. Also, there are plenty of times that one department at a bank is unaware that you paid for certain items in advance and no credits appear on the list of fees that the bank attorney will send to your lawyer. Be sure to check the fees to assure that you got your proper credit; if not, it is usually as simple as the reproduction of a cancelled check, or one phone call to straighten the situation out.

Monday, July 13, 2015—Start packing! In less than twenty-four hours, you will be a homeowner.

Chapter Notes

A Calendar of Important Events:

Property Address_____

_____

I.   1. Real Estate Binder signed on_____
        2. The cutoff date for having Contracts signed
        is_____

II.   1. Retained your lawyer on_____
        2. Delivered the binder to your lawyer
           on_____

III.   1. Retained your home inspector on

        _____

        2. The home inspector is set for_____
           at_____(a.m.) (p.m.)
        3. The inspection report will be
           ready_____
           and will be sent to your lawyer
           on_____
        4. The report revealed the following items of
           concern:

                a. _____
                b. _____
                c. _____
                d. _____
                e. _____
                f. _____

IV.   1. Contracts were signed on_____

2. A down payment check_____(check#) in
the amount of $_____was
given to your lawyer.

3. You have until _____to get a
mortgage commitment.

V.   1. You retained a mortgage professional
on_____

2. Your mortgage professional is

_____.

They are a Banker/Broker.

3. You provided your mortgage professional
with the following documents:

a. _____

b. _____

c. _____

d. _____

e. _____

f. _____

g. _____

h. _____

The following documents are still required:

a. _____

b. _____

c. _____

d. _____

e. _____

f. _____

4. I received my Good Faith Estimate, Loan Application, and Truth in Lending Form on_____

5. I delivered my Good Faith Estimate, Loan Application, and Truth in Lending Form on_____

VI. **1. The appraisal was done on**_____
2. The results of the appraisal were delivered to the bank on_____

VII. **1. The title report was received and reviewed by your lawyer on**_____
2. The following issues were highlighted by your lawyer:

  a. _____
  b. _____
  c. _____
  d. _____
  e. _____

VIII. **1. You received your mortgage commitment on** _____
2. The following conditions still need to be satisfied:

  a. _____
  b. _____
  c. _____
  d. _____
  e. _____
  f. _____

IX.   1. Your file is marked "clear to close" on

_____

X.   1. You bind your insurance on
      _____and send a copy to your lawyer
      on_____

XI.   1. You call the following to make
      arrangements:
         a. Movers on_____
            To move on_____
         b. Electric Co. on_____
            To start service on_____
         c. Water Co._____
            Service on_____
         d. Cable on_____
            Service on_____
         e. Gas Co. on_____
            Service on_____
         f. Telephone Co. on_____
            To move on_____

XII. 1. The walk through took place on_____
      2. The following issues were noted:
         a. _____
         b. _____
         c. _____
         d. _____

XIII. 1. Appointment with your lawyer for_____
      to go over the final checklist.
      2. Closing is set for_____

XIV. 1. After closing, you received your lawyer's closing statement on_____

2. You received the recorded deed on_____

3. You received the original title insurance policy on_____

4. **FIRST MORTGAGE PAYMENT DUE:**

_____

Chapter 7: The Closing

Well here it is. The day you have been waiting for has finally arrived—YOUR CLOSING. All of the years of working hard, of saving, of dreaming about this day will culminate in home ownership before the day is done. You will discover what the past several whirlwind months have been leading up to.

My experience in talking with people who have bought homes is that, after the closing has been completed, they had no idea what occurred in the two hours that took place prior to them getting their keys. This is, in part, because they were so nervous; however, it is largely due to the fact that what occurs is so confusing. This chapter will try to help you make sense of what occurs so that you can appreciate and understand the chaos a little better.

The first thing that you need to do is make sure that you are prepared for the closing. Preparation will not only insure that your closing goes off without a hitch; it will also make you feel more confident going into the closing.

As we discussed earlier, if you haven't done your walk through the night before the closing you should do it the morning of the closing. Under no circumstances should you attend the closing without having done the walk through. There is a legal theory known as *merger*, which applies to a real estate closing. In simple terms, once you accept the keys to your new home your legal relationship with the sellers is over. If the roof were to spring a leak the day after the closing you would have no legal recourse against the sellers. This theory is designed to allow people to move on with their lives without being encumbered by matters of their prior sale. The application of this theory is also a product of the difficulty of determining with certainty the time and the cause of any defect. Rather than trying to determine whether a defect predated the closing date or post dated the closing the law draws a figurative line in the sand on the day of the closing. Therefore, it is essential that you have examined the house before the closing to determine if there are any issues to address with the seller; it will be your last opportunity to do so.

You should gather a few essential items for the closing. These include:

1) Two forms of identification, preferably one with a photo.
2) Black pens.
3) Any certified checks that were requested.
4) Your personal checkbook for paying any miscellaneous items.

5) Directions to the closing location, together with a telephone number for the bank attorney, in the event you get lost.

6) Any items that your mortgage professional requested you bring. Sometimes your mortgage professional will request that you update pay stubs, or bring original documents to the closing.

7) Your original insurance binder and paid receipt.

8) A list of any problems discovered at the walkthrough.

9) Any questions you might have.

Try to arrive at the closing a few minutes early to allow yourself to get situated and comfortable before the action begins. In the event the sellers and their lawyer arrive before your lawyer does, try to avoid discussions of substance regarding the transaction. In the event that there are issues to discuss, save them for when the closing begins, and leave them to your lawyer to handle; that is what you are paying her for.

As the parties begin to assemble you will find yourself escorted to a room with a large conference table, several phones, a copy machine and a fax machine. All of the major players will begin to arrive and fill up this large room, including your lawyer, the sellers and their lawyer, the bank attorney, the title closer, the loan officer, and the real estate agents. Despite the presence of all parties, you will be the star of this entire production. You will find that the center of activity and the focus of all of the attention is on you. This is not your imagination; it is not the product of the fact that you are nervous. The focus will really be on you. This is because you serve the important function of being the borrower of the mortgage, as well as the purchaser. But for your efforts and financial wherewithal this event transaction could not have happened.

After all of the pleasantries have been dispensed with you will finally get down to business. The bank's attorney will hand your lawyer a frightening stack of legal documents for you to review and sign. These comprise the documents that the lender has required in order to secure their interest in the property. It is not necessary for you to read every word of the documents. Once again, this is why it is important to have a competent real estate lawyer. Your lawyer should be fully familiar with the contents of the documents and be able to fully explain them to you. In advising you that you do not have to read every word of every document I am not admonishing you against asking questions about the terms of the loan. You are going to be more familiar with the terms of the loan than your lawyer will, since you dealt directly with the mortgage professionals. If they do not match what you were promised, inform your lawyer of the discrepancies and she will look into it immediately.

Of the documents that you sign, the most important are the **Note,** the **Mortgage,** and the **Hud-1 Settlement Statement.** The **Note** is the document that specifies the loan amount, the interest rate, the monthly payment amount, the monthly payment rate, whether the loan is fixed or adjustable, whether there is a pre-payment penalty, and what charges will be incurred if you are late on your monthly payment.

The **Mortgage** is the security instrument that gets filed with the local County Clerk's office to put the world on notice that this lender has an interest in your property. Although the term "Mortgage" is used to describe the entire transaction, this one document is the actual Mortgage instrument. When a property is foreclosed on, it is the terms of mortgage that is utilized to accomplish this task. When the bank wants to sue you personally to recover the amount lent to you it would utilize the Note.

The **Hud-1 Settlement Statement** is a standard form utilized in financial real estate transactions that itemizes the costs associated with the transaction.

While you are busy signing until your arms are numb do not be surprised to see the sellers doing very little. The transaction is structured to be very heavily loaded in favor of the buyers doing a great deal of work and the sellers doing very little. After all, you are borrowing a great deal of money and forming a relationship with a lender that may last thirty years; the sellers are merely at the closing to drop off the keys and pick up some checks.

Once you have completed the bank and title documents you can relax while the lawyers begin to discuss "numbers", or the amount of money that you owe the sellers. The lawyers will talk about adjustments, which are, simply, accounting for the financial obligations that you and the sellers have to each other respectively for taxes, water, rents, and fuel. Real estate taxes accrue all year regardless of who owns the house. There is no final bill assessed when you transfer your property. Therefore, on the date of closing there will be some taxes that the seller has prepaid and there will be some taxes due that the seller has yet to pay. While the formulas for calculating adjustments are unimportant for our purposes here, what is important is you only pay the expenses associated with the house for the days after your closing, and the sellers pay all of the expenses that preceded the closing. Your lawyer will review the final numbers with you and answer any of your questions.

The bank attorney will review with your lawyer what expenses are being deducted from your loan. The bank attorney will also ask your lawyer for a list of expenses that your lawyer wishes to have cut directly from your loan. It is customary to have the bank attorney pay all of your various expenses out of your loan. Traditionally, you would have been given a list of numerous certified checks to bring to the closing to pay all the expenses associated with the closing. This was very confusing; the buyer would have the burden of making sure you have all the checks and that all of the names were spelled correctly. It was also costly. Most banks charge excessive fees for obtaining certified checks and you would be faced with, sometimes, certifying nearly a dozen checks. This method, invariably, led to problems and confusion, albeit, rarely of major proportions.

The modern method of deducting all of your expenses from your loan simplifies matters greatly. The way it works is simple. If your loan is for $150,000.00 and your closing costs are $10,000.00, the bank attorney would deduct the $10,000.00 from the gross loan amount, leaving the sum of $140,000.00 for use by the sellers. Therefore, your lawyer will utilize the net loan amount of $140,000.00, together with the amount you still owe the sellers to calculate the one certified check you will need to bring to the closing. This is simpler, more cost effective, and avoids any chaos over whether or not you obtained the correct checks with the payee's names spelled correctly.

After all of the numbers have been calculated and provided to the bank attorney there will be an opportunity to address any remaining issues between the parties. If there were items that came up during the walk through that you wish to address, this would be the appropriate time. You may wish to call your lawyer out of the room to discuss your concerns. In this way you can speak freely and your lawyer can provide you with her analysis of your legal position regarding these issues. The important thing is to keep your cool and allow your lawyer to do her job. Do not get into an emotional confrontation at the table. Most issues can be dealt with after a discussion, and some compromise. Remember, everyone has put a lot of time, money and effort into this transaction; everyone wants to see it close. Therefore, no matter how resistant the sellers might seem to discussing any last minute details they, probably, are not likely to be stubborn enough to walk away from the deal. My experience dictates that only a very small percentage of deals make it all the way to the closing table and do not actually close due to disagreements of the parties.

After any issues of contention are settled, there may be a period of discussing the "nuts and bolts" surrounding the house. This is a time to go over any last minute questions you have for the sellers. You may want to remind yourself of where the water shut off valves are, or what the current alarm code is, or which keys fit which doors. You should also be sure to exchange telephone numbers with the sellers in case you have any future questions and obtain their new mailing address in case you receive mail that should have been forwarded to the sellers' new address.

There will be a short period when all of the professionals will be committed to reviewing their assorted paperwork to assure that they have not forgotten something in all of the confusion; which is very easy to do, even for a seasoned professional.

Finally the bank attorney will emerge with the long awaited checks to pay all of the expenses and, most importantly, checks representing the remaining balance due to the sellers. This is the climax of the entire event; it marks the actual transfer of the consideration to the sellers in exchange for good and right title to the property, as well as the keys. It can be a very emotional moment for all involved. I remember when I bought my house; the couple I bought from had lived there for thirty years, had raised their children there, and was now retiring to Florida. They cried. Everyone hugged and congratulated each other on what had been accomplished.

You will leave the closing with very little indication of your ownership of the house, aside from an enormous debt and writer's cramp. You should leave the closing with, at the very least, a copy of the Deed to the property and the keys to the house. Your Deed may be needed to enroll your children in school, or to obtain a library card, or to finalize your service orders with various utilities.

As you walk out of the closing room you will probably be somewhat overwhelmed although you may not be sure why. The reality of your home ownership may not have "sunk in" yet. It is not uncommon to become so engrossed in the process of making that dream of home ownership that you began so many months ago come true that you lose sight of the ultimate goal. The process is so intricate, so involved, so detail oriented that it is easy to forget the romantic ideal that led you to want your own home to begin with. Well, now that dream has been fulfilled. You are a homeowner; an achievement most Americans aspire to, but only very few are able to actually achieve. Even if only for the moment, or at least until the first mortgage payment is due, you should take some time to return to the ideals that led you to want to own a home of your own to begin with.

CLOSING CHECKLIST

Closing Date_____Closing Time_____

<u>Closing Location</u>

Name: _____
Address: _____
Phone: _____

_____1. Two Forms of Identification
_____2. Black Pens
_____3. Certified Checks
_____4. Personal Checkbook
_____5. Original Insurance Binder
_____6. Original Mortgage Conditions (if any)
_____7. Walkthrough Trouble List (if any)

Any Issues You Wish to Bring Up at The Closing

1._____
2._____
3._____
4._____
5._____

Chapter 8:   What Next?

Well the wait is over. You are now the owner of your new home. It would be nice to be able to end this tale with a "and they lived happily ever after" ending. It is possible to have this fairy tale ending, but it is not a foregone conclusion. There are some important things that you can keep in mind as you enter this entirely new stage of your emotional and financial life. These considerations will help make the ending of this tale a happy one, for certain.

As we discussed earlier in this book, owning your own home is a major commitment. It is also, usually, a long-term commitment. This is important to keep in mind. There will be numerous tasks, projects, and renovations that you will wish to undertake in your new home. There is no need to do everything all at once. Many new homeowners make the mistake of spending whatever money they have left over after the closing on repairs and renovations. They leave themselves no capital reserve. This is a dangerous predicament. You should always maintain some reserve for a "rainy day". You will really appreciate money in reserve if you run into a rough spot, financially, and have to tap into your reserves to help pay the mortgage. To spend all of your reserves to create a beautiful house that you can't afford to keep would be a great shame.

Similarly, don't make the mistake of keeping money in capital reserve but "maxing" out every credit line you have to do the same renovations and repairs. Adding excessive, high interest rate credit card debt to your financial portfolio could cause you to spiral downward into financial trouble. There is a delicate financial balance that must be achieved after you purchase your home; the stakes are too high to take lightly. Credit should be utilized only when you can afford to pay the bill the next month that it comes due, or in the event of an emergency. Don't forget, you may not have had any trouble paying your credit cards before, but you did not have a mortgage then.

You need to prioritize the projects that you are considering into what needs to be done now versus what you want to accomplish eventually with the house. These projects should be divided into two distinct categories based upon the need and the cost. Of course, there will be some items that must be done in order to make the house livable. There will also be some projects that are cosmetic, but are relatively inexpensive, and can be handled with relative ease. Remember, now that you own a home you are not under any time constraints to accomplish your goals. Attack one project at a time on an ongoing basis. You will be amazed at how much you can accomplish without taking a real financial hit.

It is also important that you keep a careful accounting of your spending practices. Once again, it is a matter of establishing priorities. Your housing costs are among the largest and most important bill you will have to pay every month; prepare accordingly. Budget yourself around the date and amount of your monthly mortgage payment. This bill must be among your most important financial priorities every month. The consequences of letting yourself neglect the mortgage payment are foreclosure and the eventual loss of the house you worked so hard to earn. Even if it means foregoing other bills I would suggest making sure your mortgage is current. It is very easy, if you fall behind, to let the obligation get ahead of you. It is a significant debt and if you have trouble paying one month at a time imagine how hard it will be to pay multiple months together.

Your mortgage payment is also among one of the leading indicators of your credit. In order to keep your credit strong make sure your mortgage payment is on time and current. This will help you with other forms of credit and be vital to you if you ever want to refinance.

You should watch the mortgage rates after you purchase to see if you could affect a savings for yourself. The rates would have to drop below your current rate enough to make it worthwhile, and you would need enough time owning the house to allow the bank to consider you for refinance, but if the timing and circumstances are right, you could save a lot of money.

Be sure to perform all of the necessary, routine maintenance items on your house, such as bleeding the boiler yearly, maintaining the landscaping, and cleaning the gutters. If you are unsure of what other maintenance needs to be performed you could visit the public library or speak to other homeowners about what needs to be done. Performing these tasks will have two effects. The first is to keep your house in the condition that is the equivalent of a tuned up car. Maintenance will prevent the breakdown of key systems of your house, like the heating units, and save you hundreds of dollars in repair bills later on. You should calendar your repairs and maintain a log for future reference.

Maintenance will also keep your house looking good. This is essential not only for your own self-esteem, but for the neighborhood you live in. Keeping your property neat and well groomed will endear you to your neighbors and keep the property values in your neighborhood respectable. This is important, not only for your neighbors, but for you if you decide to sell later on.

You should think about how this house fits into your long-term goals. Is this the house you intend to grow old in or is it a starter house. I had a friend who told me he had a seven-year plan. He would stay in his house for seven years. This was enough time for him to engage the other components of his financial plan, which would allow him to buy a larger, more expensive, and more prestigious home. It does not matter what your plan is, so long as you have one, and conduct yourself according to it. This is not to say that your plan cannot change, but if and until it does, you can proceed sensibly.

It is also important to become more organized after you have a house. Perhaps investing in a good firebox, or safe, might not be a bad idea. You will need to gather and save volumes of documentation during your time in your home that may be important for reference. Starting with the closing papers sent to you by your lawyer you will want to have a safe place to store documents in the event that you need them. You will find yourself gathering appliance manuals and warranties, all of which need to be safeguarded. You will also be wise to save all of the receipts that relate to any significant work that you do on the house. These receipts, along with any other documents regarding the house, should be turned over to your accountant on a yearly basis to determine your tax benefit; and remember, at the beginning of this book we pointed to the tax benefits as being one of the reasons to buy instead of rent.

It is also important to defer to the professionals whenever you are unsure about issues of your home. The issues and consequences are too severe to fool around with by making uninformed decisions about your largest financial undertaking. If you have questions about your insurance call your insurance broker. If you have a question about your mortgage call the bank or your lawyer. If you have a question about your taxes call the appropriate party. The point is, simply, do not take chances with your financial well-being, especially when there are so many professionals waiting to guide you.

Finally, the most important piece of advice that I can give you is to make your house a home. Make your home a place where your family, friends, and neighbors will feel welcome. Make your home a place where, no matter where they end up, your children will always remember this place fondly. Make your home a place that you can come home to, at night, after a long day's work, and feel safe and secure and at ease. In short, remember what this home stands for in your life, and remember what it took to get you here. Make the most of it.

Chapter Notes